ILLUMINATED CREATURES

Winner of the 2022 New Women's Voices Competition

poems by

Angela Sucich

Finishing Line Press
Georgetown, Kentucky

ILLUMINATED CREATURES

New Women's Voices Series No. 172

ACKNOWLEDGMENTS

I am grateful to the following journals for first publishing these works:

"Deciduous" and "Pigeon" (alt. title, "Second Date at Waterfront Park")
Cave Wall
"A Pelican Feeding Her Young"
Viewless Wings Poetry Podcast ("Six Poets Recite")
"Hummingbird"
Touchstone Literary Magazine (The Editor's Project Series: "Poetry in Flight")
"The Giraffe and the Shark" (alt. title, "Recovery Costume")
Papeachu Press: *From the Waist Down: the body in healthcare*
    —Nominated for a Pushcart Prize
"Salamander"
Atlanta Review
    —Shortlisted for the 2022 *Atlanta Review* International Poetry Contest
"Everything I Love I Want to Consume"
Nimrod International Journal
    —Honorably mentioned for the 2021 Pablo Neruda Prize for Poetry

Publisher: Leah Huete de Maines
Editor: Christen Kincaid
Cover Art and Design: Jon Hanzelka
Author Photo: Peter Mike

Order online: www.finishinglinepress.com
also available on amazon.com

Author inquiries and mail orders:
Finishing Line Press
PO Box 1626
Georgetown, Kentucky 40324
USA

Table of Contents

PREFACE

Illuminated Creatures

Even in bestiaries
we keep our animals locked
in pages, for some texts want
ornament: gilded creatures
to pull eyes from the script, crawl
at edges in lapis blues
and reds, dragons spiraling
burnished forms inside letters,
and an illuminator
to layer them all upon
the corpus of another.
Compendiums of desire,
fear—marvels to flip through—here,
the book is opened. Where is
Wolf with the love charm in its
tail? Or Hydrus, the serpent
creeping into Crocodile's
mouth? See how their eyes reflect
the light, lanterns to read by.
Let us be swallowed by them.

EARTH

She/Wolf

For our potion: hair from a wolf's tail, bones
of snake, feather of owl. And as they warm,

stir in a pinch of fragrant need that's stone-
crushed and fresh from the mortar. Our love charms

are born the same as curses: from boiled things
and our own slow simmering. In wolf tales

there's a war between the human being
and the animal. But we have always

felt the wolf of our body, having burst
from the same cage together. They say fear

steals a man's voice if a wolf sees him first.
Maybe in a way he becomes a deer.

Stag Lesson

If you were hunting your own business
when you stumbled like Actaeon upon
bathing Diana in her nymph-tended ablutions,
what then would you have done?

Would you have stared like he stared at her,
luminous in the forest, wrapped only in wet
droplets and thin mountain air,
would you have seen that you were lost?

Would you have spoken to her:
Hey, have you seen my dogs anywhere...?
because you didn't mean to bother,
you were just passing by and she was there?

You say, no reason to zap you on the spot,
antler and hoof you into a creature of prey,
an herbivore with no time to ruminate
before being torn apart by your own mates.

You say you hang with hounds but you're on
the side of deer, let them run free; not like there's
something to be won in your oblivion:
a mortal glimpse, a transformation.

You say not me, innocent mistake. Say instead
an opportunity to know as Tiresias knew;
to write a new mythology, without hunters
or quarry, or any need to flee.

As a Mouse

...for mus is earth, whence also humus.
—*Isadore of Seville, Etymologies*

Traps we set for ourselves won't
kill quickly. I'm done with you,
a snap of steel through the air.

What remains: an animal
scurrying in the dirt, dark
organic matter, dead leaves,

woodland debris; the soil-born
creature whose liver is said
to grow with the moon. Return,

O tiny Prometheus—
if you can regenerate,
evade eagles and the coiled

spring, gnaw gold till your belly
shines, what creation awaits
us emerging from the loam?

Bear Mother

If I'd heard it as a girl
then I might have believed it—
bear cubs born formless until
mothers lick them into shape.
But the woman I am now
finds poetry in the lies
of old stories. Like those mole-
blind newborns, kept warm by their
mother's breathing, humming as
they suck, assured those furry
walls are all the world. Back then,
I might have wished to be more
defined by my own ursine
mother. I was second born,
willful. It took a lifetime
to see what my formlessness
was wanting. Not a mother's
tongue, but a den of my own
to hibernate in after
gorging all summer on books
and bees, shaking oak trees for
acorns in fall. When passing
a hollowed-out stump or cave
I start to hum, this feeling
that brings me back to that blind
cub—winter beyond the fur,
everything waiting for her.

Deciduous

So many words said
between us
go dormant.
Some trees save energy
surrendering their gold
in bright pools, branches
empty-handed, pearled with
spitting snow,
tree sorrow.

If shedding is a strategy
in how not to freeze,
teach me, bigleaf maples,
sugaring your cells, drying out
ice crystals, how to
sap cuts, let go
phantom limbs, how to
discard, slough off,
shed leaves, my postpartum hair,
clothes, masks, pretenses;

endure what's already been shed,
trees felled between us,
peeling back to the pith,
what can't be known in a kinder season
or unknown when seedtime returns;
as a deer many years in the wood
stands rock-still, or a fox sparrow,
scratching under conifers, flutter-hops
into the brush, wary
of homecomings.
Some winters change things.

The Weasel and the Basilisk

As if any creature could
conceive with the mouth, give birth
through the ear—though I'd like to
believe other weasel tales
from ancient lore: how it won't
turn to stone in a fight, how
it heals wounds with rue, sole herb
to withstand the serpent king's
marble glance. Perhaps we could
prove this part true, for it's been
like weasels and basilisks
around here, with me facing
down eyes that flatten mortal
enemies, and you whistling
and withering plants, shrinking
violence that coils into
itself. But we are not foes.
What tales might yet be told if
we do not kill what we love?

Dryads

Like trees to sun, their bodies bend the wrong
way round to reach the light: the twisted, scarred
ones suffer beautifully, have been starved,
have thirsted, stem-trunks wrenched in gusts too strong,
yet still they spiral, knowing they belong
to something, though not this place and time, barred
from fullness, rooted in terrain too hard
for thriving. Men have words, some birds have song
for forests like these—how they love a good
near broken thing to nest in; their first care
to shape what they will not let stand. But wood
in tension armors, holds one up to bear
another year of treehood, of girlhood—
though we take from their grasp the very air.

AIR

Ornithomancy

Soothsayers assert that the crow can represent by signs the concerns of men.
—*Aberdeen Bestiary*

However we try to tell the future—
by rain or by crow—
we look for what the soothsayers can't see
in the flap and mad flutter.

Not the ambushes.
Not the weather.
Not the movements of the sun
and the moon.

Let it be good when our bird passes
through the hall,
finds that second open door.
Let it be good.

We cast our lots long ago
in clumps of tea leaves
spirals of grain
grains of sand

cracked bone
creases in the hand
the next word on the page.
But in the darkening hour

under young stars,
the corvids lead the storks
in migration, protecting
them, they say, with their

voices of blood, while young
crows lay feathers over mothers
and fathers grown bare with age,
to keep them warm.

Such kindness is all,
and when our moment finds us,
gets under the skin, sprouts new
words the way fresh feathers

loosen old quills,
it will make space for us
to unfurl, and the birds
will call us kind.

The Caladrius

This bird is found in the court of kings. If anyone is ill, by means
of this caladrius it can be found out if he will live or die...
—*Rochester Bestiary*

I said I'd search long and far
for the white bird of legend,
learning in the end it was
there beside you all the while.
Seven years fanning your face—
you waiting for the slow drip
of chemo—leaving your side
only for trips to the sun.
Your doctor had hoped for twice
the years for you, but even
fabled birds grow tired in the
long flight to our star and back
with so much disease to burn.
Still, how your doctor would stare—
you told me once he smiled, eyes
shining glass pools, when he claimed
he could be holding your head
separated from body
like some martyred saint, and still
your head would say: *I feel great.*
See here, the caladrius
is no angel. The book of
beasts says it is an unclean
bird yet in service to kings.

I say I no longer fear
the unclean. We are decay
as much as green. Do not feel
betrayed, your bird never looked
away but drew the stream from
your eyes. That must sound like a
metaphor. But I am not
looking away, either. From
the sickness. Not the jaundice
but the gray, the wound beyond
the why. Sometimes the only
way to see something at all—
sometimes the only way to
heal something at all—let me
start again: A metaphor
is not looking away but
looking through a door. I mean,
a metaphor is looking
at a white bird, or—wait. Here,
let me have a look at you.

Pigeon, or, Second Date at Waterfront Park

A man flings crumbs
at rock doves, a child waves
her bubble wand at Puget Sound.

Beside you on the park bench
I'm keeping things light and easy
but I want to tell you how

sometimes I'm a gray dirty bird
oil slick neck bobbler
sometimes I'm waves of color

light changing with the angles
with the nacre of my inner shell,
and when crests and troughs align

my power is magnified. I want to say,
think this girl's so fragile, a soap
bubble poised to wink out?

See all the others floating up behind.
She makes herself over and over. You say
you could nab a pigeon in one swoop

I say *do it* but you don't. And I don't.
People are watching and we are not
showing things to each other yet.

Wolf Birds

Where were you when they
took our bodies?

I was sleeping, baby daughter
curled in crook of arm

soft lambkin dreaming
through a birthright lost

to black-robed birds
swooping in with the gray wolf,

beasts ever scratching for
war spoils, protectors

of their pack only; a conspiracy
of ravens. They've taken

our bodies, but the guttural croak
in this ghost throat is my own.

The Halcyon (Kingfisher)

You told me, *lucky timing*—
homebound with a newborn. *Not
missing anything,* you said
as the world closed down.

                         A bird
brooding underground still dreams
of whiplashed air, splashless dives,
the territory she shared
equitably with her pair.

Ovid wrote the winds would calm
at nesting time, kindness from
the days when even gods could
regret, make birds of lovers
they'd first slayed with thunderbolt
and grief.

                A silver lining
flashes like a minnow pinned
in an unremitting beak.

A Pelican Feeding Her Young

Illuminated folio, 13th c. Flemish manuscript

It isn't religion this
sacrificing that mothers
are expected to do. Sure,
some might plunge beak into breast
and draw forth their own blood as
pelicans were once thought to—
it isn't true, though I find
a fluid homology:
So my mother didn't nurse
me but rocked and rocked until
I slept. My own babe drinks till
I'm bloodless, while I thirst for
rest that I will never get.

Consider then the vulning
pelican—from the Latin
vulnerare, or "to wound,"
a more poetic notion
than the chewed-up fish sliding
down her chest to feed her young
(though maybe I've done that, too).
It does show the messiness
of parenting, how I have
become we, and if this is
piety, also how I
am not alone in it. Yet
the old books get it wrong when
they depict her as a fierce
eagle instead of the pouch-
neck she is. So heroic,
who can live up to it? Show
her ample gullet, how she

can still fly and hunt, provide
for her young. If a motto
flies on herald somewhere, let
it not say a pelican
"in her piety;" let it
read, "in her entirety."

The Jay, or, Where Birds Go When It Rains

Outside, the roses bend with wetness. The damp's come home,
lifting the scent of earth into the air, the house, the nose;
it will never be dry again. Water's cleansing, but how muck clings
to it, tracks dirt inside, makes a mess of every clean start.
As I walk out, the plum trees slick my arms, sodden leaves
gum to skin. I trade our musty floorboards for the promise
of the four o'clock sky: gray all day and no bone-dry certainty
of the sun's return.

glimpsed above
a broad-winged jay
bears a twig somewhere

Hummingbird

You think you are flying but
you're in your ocean again
—not seasick, never seasick
but treading the swells, body
shaking like a spray-paint can,
the mist shushing the voices,
covering all blues with blue
flowers, as you step back to
beautiful in the abstract
and far away. You need me
to tell you, you have a good
heart. It beats so quickly I
might miss it, out-sounded by
that pearly growl of wings no
one can see but must be there
vibrating infinity
at eighty times per second.
As you hover, head and chest
exposed, the feathery blur
a stillness in that golden
hour you always go back to,
you could have been anything.

WATER

Water Bear

Creation is not all big bang
it is also like
the tardigrade—
small as grains of sand
curled into a ball
hibernating its miracle
waiting for a drop of water
to expand
in clumps of moss
content to be nothing for a while
without food, water, air—
do nothing but withstand
Himalayan snow, volcano,
space beyond
the Kármán line.
What more can it do
what more can we—
but dry husk the time
and then uncurl, begin
walking in the patient gait
of the slow and small?

Aspidochelone

The poet has said, *no man*
is an island. Theseus
left his beloved on an
island. I'm waiting to see
if you and I are on an
island—the kind we're relieved
to find after treading so
much water. We reach dry land
being together, only
to see it disappear, some
deceiving hump the old tales
say sailors tied their ships to,
salt-worn seafarers never
knowing what gave its back to
loan. And how, when they lit fires
for warmth, it pulled them down, each
body a ship scuttled in
its fluking dive. Were we, too,
so trusting at the start? Our
therapist tells us not to
build foundations in the sand.
How naïve of us not to
see that everything below
the sand is unstable, too.
Maybe no one is on an
island. Maybe Theseus
left the sea a sacrifice.
I know that few people stay
together. But maybe you
and I can, if we just hold
our breath and follow the deep
plunge of our leviathan.

The Giraffe and the Shark

It's October 31st, the day after my procedure.
We spend the afternoon on a Northwest beach in costume.
You're dressed as a shark. You point a stiff fin out to sea,
as if to say, there's the place you came from and will go back to.

We spend the afternoon on a Northwest beach in costume.
But I know you are playing shark like I am playing human
as if to say, there's the place I came from and will go back to.
For now, for today, I wear a giraffe onesie to hide in.

But I know you are playing shark like I am playing human.
The costumes are borrowed. What belongs to me—
for now, for today—is a giraffe's skin to hide
a tenderness I can't stand to feel. I am not ready.

The costumes are borrowed. What belongs to me—
hands clenching yesterday's exam table, the doctor's smile,
the tenderness beneath it as she stands there asking *Are you ready?*
—all are mine behind this preposterous costume.

Too much left on yesterday's exam table, in the doctor's smile,
in what belongs to the giraffe: a long neck, head fleeing its own body
—all are mine behind this preposterous costume,
prehensile tongue picking around the thorns to find sweet leaves.

What belongs to the giraffe is a head fleeing its own body. I'd rather be
the shark that never stops moving so it doesn't sink to the bottom,
its useless tongue knowing nothing of thorns or sweet leaves.
What it knows is how to swim to breathe.

The shark never stops moving so it doesn't sink to the bottom.
It haunts the shoreline, a silent shadow with teeth for skin.
I know how to swim to breathe, I haven't forgotten.
You hold out a foam fin. I take it and become a giraffe again.

I haunt the shoreline. I know what it means to swim to breathe.
You're dressed as a shark, pointing a stiff fin out to sea.
You offer a foam fin I take in my hand. I'm a giraffe again.
It's October 31st, the day after my procedure.

The Hydrus

It lay there in the mud, an untruth,
and like all anxieties started to roll around,
getting muddier, contriving to slide into
the crocodile's mouth, take up in its stomach.
Slippery things—words and feelings, God help
us our ideas—have nothing on the hydrus,
yet manuscripts claim to have captured it:
here a water snake, there a bird, a dragon,
an otter even, for those who followed Pliny;
this thing that sneaks in while you sleep,
imagining yourself the hunter, and guts you
from the inside, leaving you in parts;
not like a birth, new life emerging,
sometimes it's just the rupturing,
showing the monster
the way out.

Naiads

We are the confluence of rivers where
one rushes to join the other and is drowned
in the rage of water and windblown hair.
We are the confluence of rivers where
mayflies live just minutes in the air
after the dance, or salmon take them down.
We are the confluence of rivers where
one rushes to join the other and is drowned.

Remora

She is attached to me constantly,
this babe I've nursed every night

for more than a year. It's enough
to make me wonder if a suckerfish

knows it is different from the shark
it rides, what matters that boundary

of body and fin. Theirs is a swift
sinuous motion inhabited together.

My own suckling's started pushing
up my shirt, laughing at both my

breasts and her good fortune I guess,
as she studies her choices, squawks

away the hand pulling at the shirt,
covering a cold nipple. Remora

the creature's called, I remember,
because I had thought it a lovely

name for a girl before I learned it
meant delay, which stole something

from that imagined child. As if she
couldn't have been the focus of some

journey but only its slowing down,
a holding back. I wonder if the shark

even feels the suction. Certainly not
the drag, though old myths claimed

remora could keep ships from sailing.
I'd read they were ground into charms

to stay childbirth until the proper time.
My own little fish squirms, latches

onto a willing surface, presses into
the shark of me, as we swim together.

Shelled

The world folds in again. Time to
huddle at the bottom, grow a rocky shell.

Friends bury themselves in sediment.
We find others to attach to, a way to be alone

together, each of us discrete and yet a reef.
Someday limestone, though we steady one

another in the wave-wash, withstanding
the company of our own gray flesh,

the staying put, the prickly sense in our
gut, the everyday needling in our mantle,

the biting worms in our side. We get by,
naming our hurts, though for her this time

it's Stage IV, she says. What can she do but
make it one more thing to curl her gloss

around, pearl the edges smooth? Pain
rounded into something else, present yet

separate. The way she encompasses it, holds
in her lustrous shell what can't be ejected.

Salamander

> *That it is possible for some living organisms to exist in the fire*
> *without being burnt, the case of the salamander clearly shows,*
> *for this creature, they say, extinguishes the fire as it walks*
> *through it.*
> —Aristotle, *History of Animals*

For too many years I was
putting out the fires he made,
taking the heat as women
have done for generations
before me, long since an
ancient physician—Galen
or maybe Hippocrates—
first described us as cold and
damp, imbalanced by nature.
A learned history, passed down
through and adhering to our
bodies. It's why we burn for
men, those old men said, being
both lustful and too frigid.
And dead tongues warned of poison
in a creature so fierce that
no flame could do it harm, but
they missed its truer feat: when torn
apart, it regrows a limb
or vital organ, one it
was always ready to lose.
A myth is a danger, too,
kept warm and intact by the
telling. Let us walk our damp
cold bodies through it again.

FIRE
(EPILOGUE)

Everything I Love I Want to Consume

The way my infant daughter squeezes her plush hippo
with her whole being, mouthing its big round nose like
a breast, leaving a wet mark the shape of her love

the way nature made a tiny chickadee the perfect size
for holding in one's mouth, if only it would sit there
calmly, carefully, nestled in its mouth-cave

the way I'd salivate, years ago, seeing my lover's
Manx kitten, big-eyed and trusting, which he had for
a time, another thing he adored and gave away

the way love can be predatory, the aunt pinching
baby cheeks she'd sooner bite, or how some mothers
thrive on pent-up energy, polishing their shields

or how I used to imagine lips wandering over objects
you'd touched, second-class relics, or the way that babies
taste everything they grasp, taking in their world

how *love* and *devour* share the same brain pathway,
a wanting rush met with the cold reminder of how close
we are from wiping away slaver to sinking in our teeth

the way poetry risks the same, rewards the same, holds
us gently, dangerously, in the mouth, lips the edges
of things, poised to kiss or bite, to consume us whole.

NOTES

In "She/Wolf," the lines "They say fear / steals a man's voice if a wolf sees him first" are adapted from the *Etymologies* of Isidore of Seville (c. 560–636): "Country folk say that a man will lose his voice if a wolf sees him first" (12, 2:23-24).

In the poem "As a Mouse," the false etymology between mouse and dirt comes from the *Etymologies*: "for *mus* is earth, whence also *humus*" (12.3.1), while the line "gnaw gold till your belly shines" is adapted from the *Natural History* of Pliny the Elder (23–79 CE): "Some kinds of mice gnaw at iron by instinct...they also gnaw at gold in mines, and when their bellies are cut open stolen gold is always found" (8, 82).

Isidore's *Etymologies* is also the source for the "The Weasel and the Basilisk" line "conceive with the mouth, give birth / through the ear," as well as its skepticism: "Some say that the weasel conceives through the mouth and gives birth through the ear, but this, says Isidore, is false" (12, 3:3). The unfounded claim about the weasel's medicinal use of rue appears in Pliny's *Natural History*, following Aristotle's *History of Animals*. Pliny asserts that: "the weasel feeds on rue, when it fights with the serpent in the pursuit of mice" (8, 41).

In the poem "Ornithomancy," the lines "Let it be good when our bird passes / through the hall, / finds that second open door" derive from Bede's *Ecclesiastical History of the English People* (8th century). In Book 2, Chapter 13, a retainer of King Edwin of the Northumbrians gives a speech comparing human life to a bird's passage through a warm hall in wintertime. In the speech, the bird (notably a sparrow instead of a crow) is described as "flying in at one door and immediately out at another," returning to the winter from which it came. References to the crows' "voice[s] of blood" and their tender care of their fathers and mothers come from Part VI of Bartholomew Anglicus' 13th-century *Mediaeval Lore*.

The art referenced in the poem "A Pelican Feeding Her Young" is from an illuminated folio in a 13th-century Flemish bestiary (Ms. Ludwig

XV 4, fol. 75). Similar depictions of pelican mothers with their chicks can be found in numerous other bestiaries. The line "a pelican in her piety" originated with the motif of the pelican in the act of self-wounding to feed/revive her chicks. Popular in medieval heraldry as well as in the characteristically moralizing bestiaries, the image was allegorized as Christ's sacrifice for humanity.

The line, "*no man is an island,*" in the poem "Aspidochelone" is taken from "Meditation XVII" of John Donne's *Devotions upon Emergent Occasions* (1624). References to the giant sea creature's masquerading as a false island that disappears beneath the disembarked sailors come from the Latin B version of the Greek *Physiologus* (possibly 2nd century CE).

Angela Sucich lives and writes in Leavenworth, Washington, ancestral land of the Yakama, Chinook, and Wenatchi people. Her debut poetry chapbook, *Illuminated Creatures* (Finishing Line Press, 2023) won the 2022 New Women's Voices Chapbook Competition and was a finalist for the 2022 Saguaro Prize and honorably mentioned for the 2022 Cutbank Chapbook Contest.

Her poems and short prose have appeared in such journals as *Nimrod International Journal, Cave Wall, Atlanta Review,* and *Whale Road Review*, and in the anthologies *From the Waist Down: the Body in Healthcare* (Papeachu Press, 2022) and *Rooted2: The Best New Arboreal Nonfiction* (Outpost19, 2023). Nominated for two Pushcart Prizes, a Best New Poets, and an Orison Books Best Spiritual Literature Award, she was honorably mentioned for the Pablo Neruda Prize for Poetry in 2021 and the Francine Ringold Award in 2020.

She holds a PhD in Medieval Literature. Her dissertation, entitled "Monstrum Partibus: Composing Hybrids in the Middle Ages" (University of Washington, 2007) reflects her ongoing fascination with monsters and how they help us understand and change the world. She's taught writing and literature courses at multiple academic institutions and spent twenty years as a freelance copywriter, editorial writer, and ghostwriter. She published a history book on a Seattle trade union before becoming a poet. Her husband and young daughter continue to inspire her poetry and her life. When she's not writing, she is most often riding a mountain bike, hiking in the hills, or paddling the river.